UTTERLY UNBEL!EVABLE

World War II

Adam FROST

Illustrated by Daniel Limon

PUFFIN

Hi, I'm Rip, a real search-and-rescue dog. I was used in the Second World War to find people trapped under bombed buildings in London.

But guess what? I'm also **TOP DOG** when it comes to sniffing out **FASCINATING FACTS**.

HOME FRONT

Let's start at home. I've dug up dozens of **TOTALLY TRUE** stories about everyday life during the war. Unlike most other wars, the Second World War didn't just affect those in uniform. Children, old people and even animals like me found that ordinary life had become extraordinary . . .

DISMAL DINNERS

The Second World War saw the arrival of food rationing.
British people were forced to get creative . . .

Squirrel-tail soup

This was one wartime speciality.
If you couldn't catch a squirrel,
then roast hedgehog was also
a prickly possibility.

A carrot on a stick

Ice cream was banned in the UK
in 1942. So kids were given this
as an after-dinner treat instead.

Crow pie

Four-and-twenty blackbirds
baked in a pie? According to
the government, this fowl
food was fabulous.

RIP'S TIPS 🐾

What was food rationing?

Just like today, in the 1930s a lot of Britain's food came from other countries. During the war, boats bringing this food were targeted by German submarines. This meant that some ingredients weren't available and others had to be limited by the government, using food coupons.

Sheep's head soup

One child remembers 'the teeth staring out from the stew, mixed with all potatoes and carrots'. Others remember seeing the brains leak out. Sounds **BAA**-baric!

Cow's udders

Although this dish had been a favourite of the Ancient Romans (they liked pig's udders, too), it was **MOO**-ved off the menu – until the war brought it back.

FEEDING TIME AT THE ZOO

Some people took experimenting with food to extremes. L. R. Brightwell, an animal anatomist and illustrator, persuaded London Zoo to give him their animals when they died (of natural causes).

But which of these animals did Mr Brightwell **NOT** try eating?

coypu

giraffe

camel

poison-dart frog

crocodile

porpoise

Answer on next page . . .

elephant

HUNGER PAINS

The lack of food affected all areas of life.

Vegetables were grown everywhere: in back gardens, in parks and next to train tracks. Sheep grazed on football fields.

Hoof it, son!

Russia under siege

Many countries suffered from far worse shortages than the UK. During the siege of Leningrad in Russia, people were forced to eat sawdust, wallpaper paste, grass and leather belts to survive.

You could go to **PRISON** for wasting food. One woman, Mary Bridget O'Sullivan, was fined £10 (over £500 today) for feeding leftover bread to the birds in her garden.

Oh, crumbs!

DID YOU KNOW?

Onions were so rare in the Second World War that they were given out as raffle prizes or birthday presents.

Answer: Mr Brightwell didn't eat the poison-dart frog. It would have killed him in minutes. He did eat the other animals, though.

WORLD WAR WHAT NOW?

So what was World War Two anyway?
And which countries were involved?

EUROPE AND NORTH AFRICA

September 1939

On 3 September 1939, Britain and France declared war on Germany after it invaded Poland. Germany had already taken over Austria and part of Czechoslovakia.

Summer 1942

The Nazis had overrun most of Europe and North Africa. Spain, Switzerland, Sweden and Ireland remained neutral. Britain was now isolated.

May 1945

By the summer of 1945, the Allies were in control of Europe. The Nazis had surrendered, and the Soviet Union and the other Allied Powers would divide Germany in two.

KEY   Allies   Axis   Neutral countries

SOUTH EAST ASIA

September 1939

Japan had taken over Korea in 1910 and invaded Manchuria in 1931. In 1937, they began a full-scale invasion of China.

Summer 1942

Japan overran European colonies in South East Asia, including French Indochina and Burma. In February 1942, the Japanese took Singapore.

August 1945

US forces and other Allied troops 'island hopped' their way to Japan. After the US dropped two atomic bombs on Japan, the War in the Pacific ended.

The main Allied powers were the UK, France, the US, China and the Soviet Union. The main Axis Powers were Germany, Italy and Japan. However, soldiers from Australia, Canada, India and dozens of other countries all played a huge role in the War.

THE BRUTAL BLITZ

The war brought about widespread bombing of towns and cities all over Europe. In Britain the German bombing campaign was called the Blitz.

London was bombed for 57 consecutive nights from 7th September to 2nd November.

The bombing only stopped (briefly) because a heavy fog on 3rd November stopped the German planes from getting through.

In Southampton, a cold-storage depot was hit. Locals remember the High Street 'running with melted margarine and butter'.

Most people hid from bombs in air-raid shelters. But in Stockport up to 6,500 people would shelter every night in a tunnel drilled into the cliffs.

As well as the bombs that went off, there were also the bombs that **DIDN'T**.

One in ten bombs dropped in the UK and Germany didn't explode.

There are still unexploded bombs today. German bomb-disposal teams find and defuse a World War Two bomb every **TWO WEEKS**. And it's been over 70 years since they were dropped!

Worst teacher ever?

Only four kids in one Bristol class made it into school after a night of bombing. When they explained that they hadn't done their homework, the teacher said the war was no excuse and gave them all detention!

WHEELER DEALER

During the war, a lot of goods were hard to come by. In the UK, criminals called 'spivs' would offer black-market goods . . . for a price.

Clothes were a common black-market product. Spivs would sell clothes and forged clothing coupons.

Most food was rationed. By 1945, 38% of eggs were sold via the black market.

As well as stolen cosmetics, spivs would also sell their own concoctions – like face powder made from chalk, and foundation made from margarine.

Rabbits and other wild animals were poached and sold.

Some particularly vile villains would sell watches and jewellery that they'd stolen from dead bodies.

13

HOUSE GUESTS

Over two million British children were evacuated to the countryside during the Second World War. They had to get used to a new way of life . . .

Some city children had only ever slept on the floor. One country family lost their evacuee and found him asleep under the bed because that's where he slept at home.

Some city children stayed in the same clothes all day and all night. One village teacher from Chepstow remembers: 'A little girl said she always went to bed in her frock and didn't know what a nightgown was.'

A lot of city children rarely bathed. One evacuee screamed when he saw a bath full of water – he thought he was going to be drowned!

Many evacuees didn't have toilets at home. One head teacher complained: 'What can be done with a child who goes into the corner of the drawing room instead of the lavatory?'

Evacuees were often only allowed to take **ONE TOY** with them in their suitcase. Which toy would **YOU** take?

Farm animals were another new experience. Two boys from Glasgow were terrified of a cow. Another evacuee, Reg Baker, thought a hedgehog was a hairbrush!

What was an evacuee?

An evacuee was someone moved from a town or city, during the war, to a rural location (which was less likely to be bombed). Evacuees were mostly children, and they tended to be from poor city families. They rarely knew the people they were sent to stay with.

All aboard

Evacuees shared their journeys with some strange passengers.

Sick people

There could be up to 10 stretchers in each train carriage as all the London hospitals were evacuated.

Animals

In 1940, cows and other farm animals were evacuated from farms that were too close to built-up areas.

Pleased to meet you!

Are you my mum?

Some evacuees were away for five or six years, and their parents didn't always recognize them when they returned home. Joyce Withers said her name was printed on her suitcase and she held it up at the station. Two adults she didn't recognize claimed her. 'Here I was saying hello to a family I didn't know at all and they didn't know me,' she remembers.

A success story

Evacuation might have been hard for some kids – but it worked. Only 27 evacuees from London died in air raids. **THOUSANDS** of children who stayed in the cities lost their lives.

UNDERGROUND ART

When the Nazis marched through Europe, they stole hundreds of valuable paintings for Hitler's planned 'super museum' in Austria.

The UK prepared itself for possible invasion by **HIDING** its most valuable art in **TOP-SECRET** locations.

Pictures from the National Gallery in London were hidden underground in a slate mine in Wales.

Stanley Spencer's painting *The Resurrection, Cookham* was too gigantic for the Tate Gallery to move. So they built a brick wall in front of it.

The priceless Stone of Scone was moved from Westminster Abbey to a mystery location. Then the 'treasure map' was sent to the Prime Minister of Canada to keep it safe.

Perhaps the strangest story of **HIDDEN VALUABLES** relates to a British scientist called **ALAN TURING** . . .

TURING'S TREASURE

Alan Turing was one of the cleverest men who ever lived. But even the smartest people can make silly mistakes . . .

It's 1940 and Alan Turing is hard at work at Bletchley Park, trying to crack the cunning codes that the Germans use to send messages to each other.

To do this, he built an early computer called a bombe . . . that could decrypt even the trickiest messages.

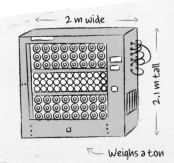

By the end of the war, with the help of other brilliant codebreakers, Turing had built 211 bombes.

All 211 bombes were destroyed after the war to keep their existence secret.

Historians have estimated that these code-cracking machines shortened the war by around two years saving 14 million lives.

Turing's work would also lay the foundation of modern computing. Without Turing, there'd be no mobile phones and no computer games!

It's fair to say that Alan Turing was unique.

In springtime, he wore a gas mask outdoors. This was to stop himself getting hay fever.

He chained his mug to the radiator to stop anyone stealing it.

When he had meetings in London (40 miles away), he liked to run there.

But perhaps the strangest thing about this truly exceptional man was the way he chose to hide his money.

In 1940, when he thought the Germans were going to invade, he converted all his money into two large silver bars.

worth £250 in 1940 (about £13,000 now)

He put these bars in a pram . . .

Hello, precious!

. . .and wheeled it out into the countryside around Bletchley Park.

Then he dug a big hole and buried the silver . . . writing the location down in code.

Can you guess what happened next?

a) He forgot where he buried the silver bars.
b) When he dug them up, they'd gone rusty, making them worth almost nothing.

Answer on next page . . .

CHANGING ROOMS

The war meant that British people's homes looked completely different. Take a look at how this typical home in a London suburb was transformed by war.

BEFORE

Answer: a) He forgot where the silver bars were. They could still be in Bletchley Park today . . .

AFTER

Can you spot what's changed in the two pictures? There are **TEN BIG DIFFERENCES**.

Answers on next page . . .

ANSWERS

1

People donated their pans to the war effort. Government leaflets suggested that for every 5,000 pans, they could make one fighter plane.

2

It was curtains for fancy curtains! In cities, people had to put up blackout curtains so that not a single chink of light escaped.

3

Could you face wearing one of these? Everyone was issued with a gas mask and you were meant to carry it everywhere.

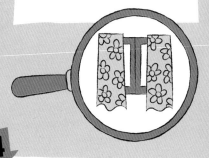

4

Tape was stretched across window glass so that, if a bomb exploded outside, the people inside wouldn't be cut by broken glass.

5

To save on fabric, boys had to wear short trousers until the age of 12.

6

No patterns were allowed on plates as it was seen as a waste of factory workers' time.

7

Meat was rationed so the Sunday roast was toast! There were no restrictions on vegetables like potatoes and carrots, though.

8

From 1942 you couldn't make tablecloths any more – because the fabric was needed for uniforms and equipment.

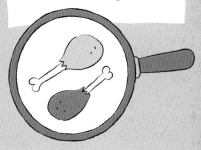

9

In the war, newspapers could be half the size or even smaller. Every type of paper was rationed and wrapping paper was completely banned. Birthday presents weren't much of a surprise!

10

School was out! Many schools, especially in cities, were closed. And if you did go to school, you didn't always learn much. Roy Bartlett remembers one school day after a bombing raid: 'Myself and some others had dozed off. I awoke, looked up and saw that the teacher was asleep too.'

THE GREAT OUTDOORS

What would you have seen if you'd looked out of the window of a London suburban home in the war?

Answers on next page . . .

25

ANSWERS

1

Barrage balloons filled the London skies. The balloon cables were designed to catch German dive bombers and cause them to crash.

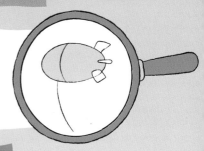

2

From 1940 churches were no longer allowed to ring their bells. Instead they were only to be rung as a signal that the Germans had invaded.

3

In 1941 a new law allowed the government to pull up and melt down any iron railings built after 1850. They used the metal for weapons and vehicles.

4

Pets could wear gas masks, too! The 5th Marchioness of Exeter had a gas mask made for her sheepdog, Roy.

5

Shop signs and signposts were removed and painted over so, if German parachutists landed, they wouldn't know where they were.

When bombs exploded, the explosion sometimes covered nearby trees with strange objects. One family remembers seeing a tree in their back garden full of cabbages from their vegetable patch.

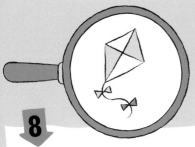

7

Lamp posts had sandbags beneath them. The sand was meant to be poured on incendiary bombs to stop them causing fires.

8

Toys were in short supply. Kites were banned because they could be used to signal to the enemy. Fireworks could be mistaken for weapons and had to be handed into the authorities.

9

From 1942 only essential vehicles were allowed petrol, so the number of cars on the road dropped. New cars stopped being made: the USA made over 3,000,000 cars in 1941, but only 139 during the rest of the war.

10

Lamp posts were switched off or masked. Cars had masks fitted over their headlights to reduce the amount of light, and their bumpers were painted white.

NAZI OR NUN?

In 1940 a German invasion of Britain was widely expected. In this feverish atmosphere, one **RUMOUR** became hard to shift. The Germans would arrive . . . dressed as nuns.

In the summer of 1940 there were rumoured sightings of German parachutists dressed as nuns descending on the British countryside.

Sister act

One Lancashire schoolboy, Chris Boyd, remembers 'eyeing all nuns with suspicion'. Another child, Barbara, remembers secretly peering at nuns' shoes in case they were wearing German-made boots.

I'm pure of sole!

Heavily armed

The author Virginia Woolf heard a rumour that German spies dressed as nuns travelled on London buses – usually in pairs. You could spot them by their hairy arms as they stretched out to pay for a ticket.

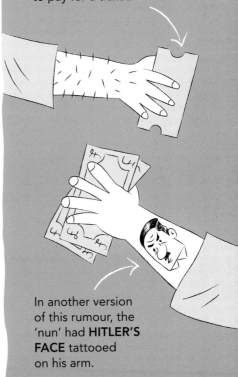

In another version of this rumour, the 'nun' had **HITLER'S FACE** tattooed on his arm.

But maybe the stories weren't all silly. One **BRITISH** spy, Margaret Spencer, admitted in 2014 that **SHE** had parachuted behind enemy lines dressed as a nun. And the disguise worked!

RIDICULOUS RUMOURS

But it wasn't just the rumour of Nazi nuns that got people worked up . . . .

Here's how an actual rumour travelled in a town in Cornwall during the war.

DAY 1 — There are soldiers on the beach using a BUOY for target practice.

DAY 2 — Soldiers shot a BOY while he was playing on the beach.

Whisper Whisper

DAY 3 — A German aircraft machine gunned 60 BOYS while they were playing on the beach.

Other strange rumours included:

Germans were going to drop a chemical that made your gas mask melt into your face.

Germans were dropping poisoned sweets out of aeroplanes for children to pick up.

All of these rumours were **RUBBISH!**

CHANGING COLOURS

During the war, familiar objects could take on a strange complexion . . .

Before

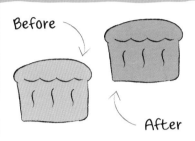

After

Due to a lack of high-quality white flour, the traditional British white loaf ended up looking grey in the war. It was also deliberately sold a day late: if it was a bit stale, then people wouldn't eat it all at once.

Before   After

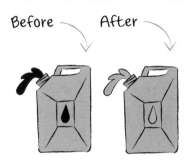

Official petrol was dyed red. Petrol was rationed and ordinary people weren't supposed to use it, so if a police officer saw you using **RED** petrol, you'd get arrested.

Before

After

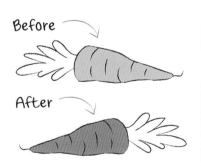

Some carrots were used as animal feed. These were sprayed purple to show that they were meant for animals and not people.

Before

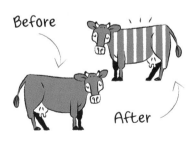

After

Some farmers painted white stripes on their cows, so they were more visible during the blackout. If they wandered on to the road, drivers would see them.

WHAT A STITCH-UP!

During the war, clothes were rationed in most countries. By 1945 everyone in the UK had 24 coupons a year to spend on clothes. Time for our Cunning Clothes Coupon Challenge!

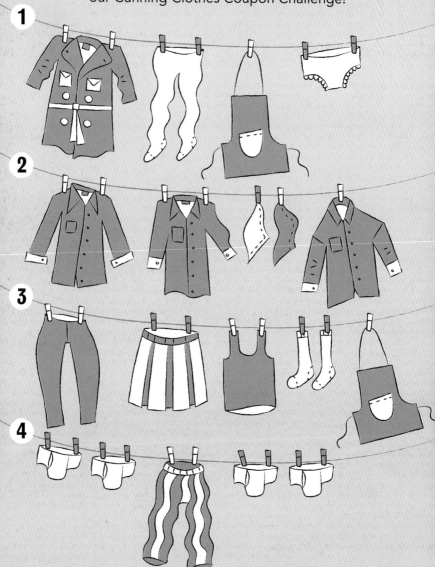

NUMBER OF COUPONS REQUIRED

MEN

 Overcoat (16)

 Trousers (8)

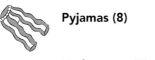 Shirt (8)

 Pyjamas (8)

 Underpants (4)

 Socks (3)

WOMEN

 Dress (11)

 Skirt (7)

 Vest (3)

 Apron (3)

 Knickers (3)

 Stockings (2)

 Hankerchiefs (1 coupon for 2 hankies)

The four households on the left have just been given their annual allowance of 24 coupons. But which family has used the **BLACK MARKET** to get some extra clothes? Use this (real-life!) coupon chart to help you catch the crooks.

CLUE: The clothes on the **BAD** family's washing line will add up to **MORE** than 24.

Answer on next page . . .

RIP'S TIPS

Why were clothes rationed?

Clothes were rationed during the war because material, tailors and factories were needed to make soldier's uniforms, parachutes, tents and many other war materials! Rationing was introduced to try to make sure that all civilians had their fair share of clothing.

WORLD WAR POO!

Even going to the toilet was a battle in the Second World War.

A clean sheet

If you were at home, toilet paper was in short supply. One British woman, Joan Styan, remembers getting one roll per family per week. In Germany there was no toilet paper at all.

The Daily Blah

War and Peace

Alternatives to loo roll

British soldiers were allowed **THREE** sheets of paper **A DAY**.

But the American soldiers were luckier. They were given 23 sheets a day.

Feeling the chill

The toilet situation was even worse if you were taken prisoner. There was almost never toilet paper in prison camps. One prisoner remembers using leaves, and another said he wiped his bottom with snow. Eek!

Answer: Washing line 2 is the odd one out. The clothes add up to 25!

A TOTAL WASHOUT

Bath time wasn't much fun in the war either.

For British people, this is **EXACTLY** how deep your bath was allowed to be during the war (that's only 12.7 centimetres!)

Plus, Brits were only allowed one bath a week, and you usually had to share the bathwater with your **WHOLE** family.

In Germany you could only have a bath at the weekend!

In the UK, you were given one bar of soap per family every **FOUR WEEKS**. There was no shower gel and no shampoo, so this single bar of soap had to wash everything.

12.7 centimetres (measure it!)

TOP OPERATIONS

When armies launched operations in the Second World War, they were always given **CODE NAMES**. Can you guess which of these were real names for official operations?

Operation Toenails

Operation Super Gymnast

Operation Nostril

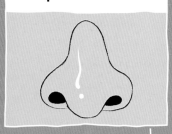

Operation Slippery

Operation Bottom

Operation Mung Bean

YES!

This was the US assault on New Georgia in the South Pacific Ocean, in 1943.

NO!

This code name is simply **TOO** ridiculous. Unlike Operation Lentil (which existed) and Operation Nibble (also real).

DEFINITELY!

This was a British plan to blow up Italian warships with midget submarines.

YES!

This was a British naval plan to destroy German ships in the Aegean Sea.

TRUE!

When the British were planning to land ships in Malaya, this was a deception operation.

TRUE!

This was the proposed plan to land British and US troops in North Africa in 1942.

OVERGROUND . . .

Some battles were fought high in the sky.

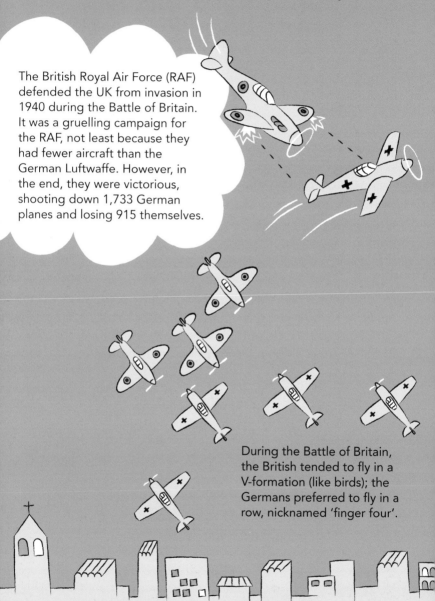

The British Royal Air Force (RAF) defended the UK from invasion in 1940 during the Battle of Britain. It was a gruelling campaign for the RAF, not least because they had fewer aircraft than the German Luftwaffe. However, in the end, they were victorious, shooting down 1,733 German planes and losing 915 themselves.

During the Battle of Britain, the British tended to fly in a V-formation (like birds); the Germans preferred to fly in a row, nicknamed 'finger four'.

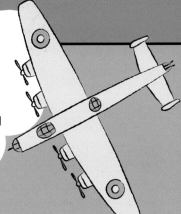

Bombers like this British Lancaster were a familiar sight in the sky. By the end of the war, Allied bombing raids had destroyed 59% of Dresden and 75% of Hamburg in Germany. The Allies suffered too – over 50% of Coventry in the UK was destroyed in a single night by bombs.

Planes also dropped parachutists behind enemy lines. One of the biggest drops was on D-Day (6 June 1944) when 17,000 Allied parachutists landed in occupied France in one night! (Find out more on page 56.)

Japanese kamikaze pilots were terrifying opponents. Around 3,600 died in suicide missions by flying planes into Allied battleships. Some of the planes carried bombs as well. Their motto was: 'One man, one ship.'

... UNDERGROUND

Some battles were fought deep underground.

Several countries' leaders directed the War from offices deep underground. The British Cabinet war rooms were three metres underground. Mussolini's bunker in Rome was six and a half metres underground, and Hitler's hideout was 15 metres under Berlin!

As the US army advanced towards Japan, Japanese soldiers dug tunnels to defend islands such as Iwo Jima. Over 18 kilometres of tunnels were dug under this tiny (four-kilometre-wide) island. A battle that the Americans hoped to win in three days took almost a month.

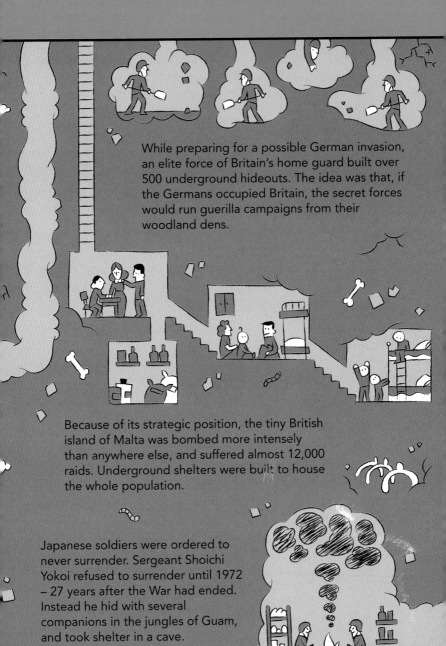

While preparing for a possible German invasion, an elite force of Britain's home guard built over 500 underground hideouts. The idea was that, if the Germans occupied Britain, the secret forces would run guerilla campaigns from their woodland dens.

Because of its strategic position, the tiny British island of Malta was bombed more intensely than anywhere else, and suffered almost 12,000 raids. Underground shelters were built to house the whole population.

Japanese soldiers were ordered to never surrender. Sergeant Shoichi Yokoi refused to surrender until 1972 – 27 years after the War had ended. Instead he hid with several companions in the jungles of Guam, and took shelter in a cave.

IN THE JUNGLE . . .

From 1942, the Allies were battling the Japanese in the jungles of Burma. As well as bullets and bayonets, there were a range of other adversaries . . .

Monsoon rain

Private Dick Fidament remembers: 'the heaviest rainfall in the world. You think to yourself, if it doesn't stop beating against my poor skull, I'll go insane.'

Diseases

Malaria and dysentery were common, and many soldiers got trench foot from the permanently muddy ground. Ivor Robert Phillips recalls how every evening 'I had to bathe my rotten foot in wee.' (Wee is an antiseptic!)

Falling bags of rice

The air force would drop parcels of food, but they wouldn't always use parachutes. Dominic Neill remembers how bags of rice 'hit the ground with a tremendous whack and would have killed any mule or soldier had they hit [them].'

Blank maps

'There was a map showing where we were going. It was absolutely white, because it had never been surveyed – nobody had ever been there,' Lieutenant Sam Horner recollects.

Leeches

Sir John Rowland recalls removing up to 600 leeches from his body every day. The worst were elephant leeches, which were over 20 centimetres long!

. . . IN THE DESERT

In June 1940 the North African campaign began when Italy declared war on the Allies. As well as avoiding landmines and tanks, soldiers faced other difficulties . . .

Extreme weather

The temperature could reach over 40 degrees Celsius during the day but drop to below zero at night. You'd need shorts and a T-shirt in the daytime and lots of layers when you slept!

Nowhere to hide

There were few towns or houses and little vegetation. Digging a trench for shelter was no fun. One soldier, Bill Hutton, remembers: 'I got a pick and shovel and it was just like rock. I hit the ground and sparks flew up from my pick.'

Mirages

The heat caused optical illusions. 'You'd see a man walking upside down fifteen foot in the air – distorted visions – you couldn't aim at it because you didn't know where he was really,' Ray Ellis recalls.

Sandstorms

Sandstorms would last for days and could cut visibility to less than 50 metres. Sand would stop your weapons and vehicles from working. Meals would be ruined as 'the last spoonfuls were sand', remembers Private Kev Robinson.

Bugs

There were flies everywhere. Plus mosquitoes and scorpions. And bugs you hadn't seen before: 'If this insect bit you, and you brushed it off, it left its head behind,' Sergeant Major Alan Potter recalls.

THE WAR UNDERWATER

During the War, humanity sank to
new depths . . .

Submarine crews had to deal with
whirlpools, huge waves and 150-mph
winds. One German submarine (or U-boat)
commander, Herbert Werner, said,
'Utensils, spare parts, tools and conserves
[food] showered down on us continually.'

U-boats hunted in 'wolf packs'.
When one U-boat spotted a
target, it would signal for others
nearby to join them. At night-time
they would surface and attack
their target together.

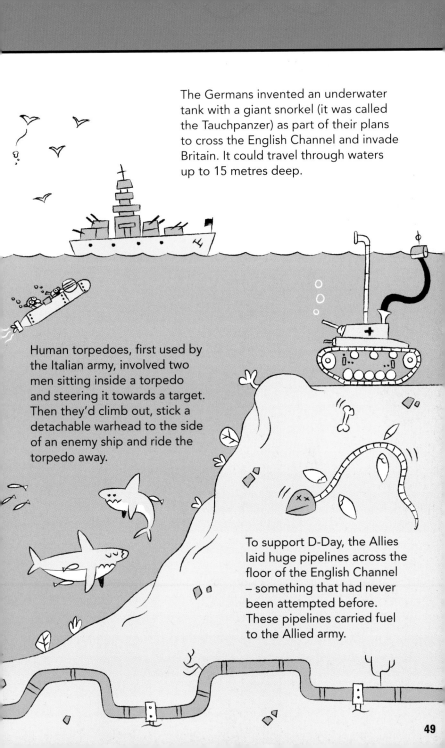

The Germans invented an underwater tank with a giant snorkel (it was called the Tauchpanzer) as part of their plans to cross the English Channel and invade Britain. It could travel through waters up to 15 metres deep.

Human torpedoes, first used by the Italian army, involved two men sitting inside a torpedo and steering it towards a target. Then they'd climb out, stick a detachable warhead to the side of an enemy ship and ride the torpedo away.

To support D-Day, the Allies laid huge pipelines across the floor of the English Channel – something that had never been attempted before. These pipelines carried fuel to the Allied army.

DON'T TELL ME WHAT TO DO!

Every soldier has to obey orders from their superiors.
But do you know who's above and who's below?
Use the ranks in the clue bar to help you!

1

In the army, does a Private have to obey a Sergeant Major?

Go and clean out the toilets!

Highest
- Sergeant Major
- Sergeant
- Corporal
- Lance Corporal
- Private

Lowest

2

In the army, does a Major have to obey a General?

A black coffee and make it snappy!

Highest
- Field Marshal
- General
- Brigadier
- Colonel
- Major

Lowest

3

In the navy, does an Admiral have to obey a Captain?

Highest
Admiral
Vice-Admiral
Rear-Admiral
Commodore
Captain
Lowest

4

In the air force, does a Squadron Leader have to obey an Air Marshal?

Highest
Air Marshal
Air Commodore
Group Captain
Wing Commander
Squadron Leader
Lowest

Answers: 1. Yes. 2. Yes. 3. No! 4. Yes.

KEEPING TRACK

In the chaos of war, people would use marks and charts to keep track of what was happening to them.

PLANE MARKINGS

This Lancaster pilot is painting roundels on the side of his aircraft, one for each successful mission.

The average number of bombing raids completed by a Lancaster (before it was shot down) was 25. The highest number of completed missions was an incredible 109!

LOST AT SEA

In 1940, the merchant ship *The Anglo-Saxon* was sunk by a German U-boat. Only two men survived and they drifted 2,500 miles over 70 days, from near the Canary Islands to Eleuthera in the Bahamas! They made notches on the side of their rowing boat to indicate how long they'd been drifting.

MARKING TIME

In prisoner-of-war (POW) camps, prisoners often used tally charts or other markers to keep track of how many days they had been in captivity.

Alfie Fripp is thought to be the longest-serving British prisoner of war, spending almost six years in 12 different German POW camps between 1939 and 1945. That's over 2,000 days!

This is 100 days – you'd need to fill 20 more walls like this to get to 2,000 days!

SAFE LANDING

During the War, children in the south east of the UK became very good at counting planes. One child, Ann, who lived near Northolt airfield remembers: 'We used to count [the planes] going out, and count them returning, always hoping it would be the same number.'

5 planes (going out) +

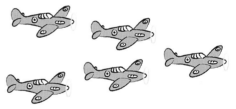

5 planes (coming back)

= all the planes made it home

DEADLY COMBAT

The biggest battles of the Second World War all took place in the biggest country – the Soviet Union. Here are two of the largest and bloodiest campaigns.

 1941 – Operation Barbarossa (the German invasion of Russia)

V.

3 million German troops
(680,000 casualties)

5.5 million Soviet troops
(2.8 million casualties)

KEY

 = 100,000 soldiers

 = 100,000 casualties
(dead or wounded)

To see ALL the major battles of the Second World War, turn to our timeline on page 106.

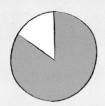

80% of Russian men born in 1923 died in the Second World War

80% of German army deaths in the Second World War happened on the Eastern Front

 1943 – Ukraine campaign (a Soviet counter-attack against the Germans)

V.

2.5 million Germans
(213,000 casualties)

6 million Soviets
(430,000 casualties)

Another huge battle happened at Kursk in Russia in 1943. It was the largest tank battle in history.

 V.

1859
German tanks

6672
Soviet tanks

KEY   1 tank icon = 1000 real tanks

D-DAY DRAMA

On 6 June 1944, 185,000 Allied soldiers landed in France in a single day. For many of them, it was the toughest ordeal of their lives.

Weeks before

First, there was tortuous training. Soldiers had to rehearse again and again. Some soldiers remember having buckets of animal organs thrown at them to imitate the experience of battle.

The day before

D-Day was originally meant to be on 5 June. But bad weather delayed the invasion by a day. Soldiers had to wait on their boats, getting more seasick. Talking of which . . .

The voyage begins

A lot of the soldiers vomited. 'The smell was vile,' recalls Sergeant Major William Brown. Many used their helmets as sick buckets.

The voyage continues

Waves were up to two metres high, covering the troops in spray and chilling them to the bone. Many used their helmets again – this time to bail out water.

RIP'S TIPS

What was D-Day?

D-Day was the first day of the Normandy landings: the Allied campaign to free Western Europe from the Nazis. It is seen as a major turning point in the War.

Approaching the beaches

The Germans opened fire. Soldiers were given wooden pegs to plug any holes that appeared in their landing craft. This was meant to stop water coming in – but it didn't always work.

The landing

The landing craft couldn't always get close to the beaches, so the soldiers had to jump into the sea. It was very cold – around 13 degrees Celsius. Some sank because of the weight of their equipment.

The luggage

The troops had to bring EVERYTHING with them – including the harbours they landed on, which they towed across the English Channel.

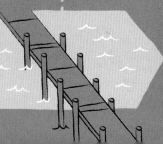

On the beach

As well as bullets, troops had to deal with German mines – everywhere. Around 100 million mines had been placed on France's beaches. If you got past those, there were rows of barbed wire and anti-tank girders.

Joining the fight

If you made it beyond the beach, you had to hope your equipment still worked. Many soldiers found that their weapons jammed because of the sand.

Trying to survive

Throughout, soldiers had to cope with fear, hunger, tiredness and grief. Private Leslie Perry remembers: 'I felt lonely, more than anything. I felt everyone was firing at me.'

In spite of these difficulties, D-Day was a military success. The Allies liberated Paris from the Germans less than three months later.

A DIFFICULT LANDING

Many paratroopers on D-Day were dropped in the wrong place – including US Private John Steele. This is his story.

Like 17,000 other parachutists, John Steele was dropped behind enemy lines on 6 June 1944 (D-Day).

His parachute became snagged on the steeple at Sainte-Mère-Église in northern France.

After two hours, the Germans took him prisoner by pulling him through the steeple window.

It took two weeks for his hearing to come back.

John!

Who's Ron?

He'd been deafened by the church bells.

He later escaped from the German POW camp and rejoined his division.

Together they recaptured the town of Sainte-Mère-Église from the Germans.

If you go to the town today, you'll see a model of John Steele and his parachute . . .

. . . still hanging from its church tower.

Broken toilets can get you into deep water . . .

In April 1945 a German submarine captain was using his brand-new high-tech submarine toilet.

He couldn't seem to flush it, so he called in an engineer. But the engineer flushed the toilet the wrong way . . .

This caused the cabin to flood with seawater and poo.

The water trickled down on to the submarine's batteries . . .

. . . which released a deadly gas.

Eventually the captain and crew had to abandon ship, and the submarine sank to the bottom of the sea.

It's the only known case in history of a leaky loo sinking a sub!

TERRIFIC TRANSPORT

As well as planes, boats and tanks, there were more
unusual ways of travelling through a war zone . . .

SKIS

In 1939, the Finnish army
used ski soldiers to attack
the invading Russians.
They would slip out of the
woods, hurl grenades or
bombs and then vanish
back into the trees.

BIKES

In 1941, the Japanese
invaded Malaya on bicycles.
They had previously used
50,000 bicycle troops during
the 1937 invasion of China.

SNOWMOBILES

Also known as aerosanis or
battle sledges, these formed
a critical part of the Russian
war effort. They were usually
powered by engines and
some had propellers.

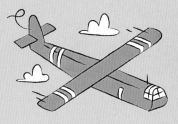

GLIDERS

These planes had no engines,
no guns and no parachutes!
Pilots had to be towed
towards their destinations by
larger planes – then they
glided for the last part of the
journey. Gliders tended to be
used in secret missions.

THE SECRET WAR

Now it's time to take a look at the secret war. This is a world of spies, double agents and undercover operations. Plus cunning canines like me!

I'm going to write the next sentence in code – just to get you in the right mood.

!YPS TAERG A EKAM DLUOW UOY

Did you crack it?

PRIVATE

WACKY WEAPONS

Jokes and pranks were a serious business
in the Second World War.

ITCHING POWDER

Allied resistance members in
laundries and factories would
sneak itching powder into
enemy uniforms – in particular
their **UNDERPANTS**. For one
German submarine crew, the
itching was so intense that the
sub had to return to base!

SUPER
SCRATCHY

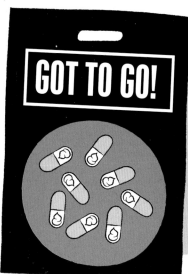

GOT TO GO!

LAXATIVES

Norwegian secret agents
sneaked croton oil into
tins of sardines that were
fed to German submarine
crews. Croton oil makes
you go to the toilet – a
LOT. Imagine everyone in
a submarine needing the
loo at the same time . . .

SUPERGLUE

Another British plan involved dropping strong glue on to German soldiers, sticking them to the ground. The war ended before this glue could be made!

STINK BOMBS

British spies developed capsules of seriously stinky slime. Secret agents would break them on to Nazi officers' uniforms to make them feel embarrassed during meetings.

EXPLODING POO

In the deserts of North Africa, the British used exploding camel droppings to blow up the tyres on Italian trucks. The (real) camel poo was supplied by London Zoo and the explosives were packed inside.

OPERATION MINCEMEAT

Our story has a sad beginning, but don't worry
– it all ends happily (for the Allies, that is.)

In 1943, a homeless man called Glyndwr Michael ate rat poison – probably by accident – and died on the streets of London.

Little did he know he was about to save millions of lives.

Glyndwr was kept in a fridge for three months, so he didn't start to decompose.

At the same time, the man who would later write the James Bond books came up with a strange idea.

The name's Fleming. Ian Fleming.

Why not drop a corpse in the sea, wearing clothes packed with **MADE-UP** government secrets?

That would be a good way of **TRICKING** the Germans.

So Glyndwr was dressed up as a pretend British Captain called William Martin.

Name:
William Martin
Rank:
Captain
Status:
Definitely real and not made-up.

In his pockets, there were letters saying the British Army would invade Sardinia and Greece and **DEFINITELY NOT** Sicily.

His body was transported by a submarine to the south coast of Spain.

They did this because Spain wasn't in the War.

Submarine's route

If they'd left it next to Germany, it would have looked **TOO** suspicious.

They also put it some distance from the shore.

Body dropped here

If they'd left it on the beach, that would also have looked **TOO** suspicious.

A Spanish fisherman found it and gave it to the authorities.

I've taken the bait!

Even though the Spanish were neutral, Britain suspected that the secrets would get passed to the Germans. And they were!

The Germans believed everything they read. They moved troops to Greece and Sardinia and **AWAY** from Sicily . . .

Sicily

The operation was a **SUCCESS**!

This proved to be a turning point: Allied troops were able to conquer Sicily in only five weeks and then they advanced into mainland Italy. (Turn to page 107 to read more!)

ANIMAL ARMY

Animals were also used in undercover operations.
But one of the stories below is a shaggy dog story.
Can you guess which one is **MADE–UP**?
Turn over for the answer!

Paradogs were used during
D-Day to sniff out mines and
warn soldiers when enemy
troops were approaching.
One dog, Rob, flew on 20
secret parachuting missions.

In 1942, a British bomber plunged
into the North Sea. Before they
crashed, the crew released Winkie
the carrier pigeon. Winkie was
covered in oil but flew 120 miles
back to her owner, who alerted the
authorities and saved the crew.

In 1940, Australia gave the British government 200
sharks to release into the English Channel, to attack
any Axis forces that tried to invade.

Siwash the duck was the mascot of the US Tenth Marine Regiment. During the invasion of Tawara, Siwash joined in the battle, attacking a Japanese rooster. Siwash received a nasty neck wound but chased the rooster away. Siwash was awarded a Purple Heart medal for bravery.

Beehives were thrown at Italian tanks by Ethiopian soldiers. They caused several tanks to tumble off course and crash.

Wojtek the bear was a private in the Polish army. He had his own pay-book and often slept alongside his fellow soldiers in their tents. In the Battle of Monte Cassino he carried crates of ammunition and didn't drop a single one.

Guten tag!

During the War, a group of German scientists claimed they had taught dogs to speak. The institute in Leutenberg said that one dog was asked who Hitler was, and reportedly barked: 'Mein Führer!'

Answer on next page . . .

A FEMALE FÜHRER

Perhaps the pottiest plan of the British secret
services involved turning Hitler into a woman . . .

★ CLASSIFIED ★

Top
Secret

British spies had spent years
working out how to smuggle
poison into Hitler's food.

But they were foiled by Hitler's
army of 15 food-tasters who
tested everything he ate.

So the Brits came up with a
different plan. What if they
bribed Hitler's gardener to
inject oestrogen into Hitler's
carrots?

Sshh! Don't tell

Answer: The shark story was made up by British intelligence.
It was hoped that it would make the Germans too frightened
to invade. They also spread a rumour that Britain had a
weapon that could set the whole sea on fire! (They didn't).
All the other animal stories are true!

★ CLASSIFIED ★

What's oestrogen? It's a hormone that helps women's bodies to develop and grow.

It's also flavourless, so it can't be tasted if it's in your food.

The idea was, if Hitler ate enough of it, he'd slowly become more like his sister, an unremarkable secretary called Paula.

He might become less interested in fighting. He might even tell the German army to surrender.

In the end, the ridiculous plot was abandoned. The Allies were able to win the War without hijacking Hitler's hormones!

Cunning plan!

It's a secret!

True or false? Another strange plan cooked up by the Brits involved sneaking exploding rats into German buildings.

Answer on next page . . .

BIG DATA

During the War a top-secret American team built ENIAC, one of the first computers. But how does ENIAC compare to modern machines?

ENIAC WEIGHT

ENIAC = 27 tonnes

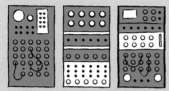

That's the same weight as

two double-decker buses.

Modern mobile phone
= 138 grams

That's the same weight as

a hamster.

ENIAC SIZE

It covered 167 square metres. That's about two-thirds of a tennis court. A modern laptop is 0.1 square metres.

☐ Tennis court
▧ ENIAC
■ A modern laptop

Answer: It is true. Brits filled dead rats with explosives and left them near boilers in German police offices. The idea was that a dead rat would get thrown into the boiler and . . . boom!

72

RIP'S TIPS

What was ENIAC?

ENIAC was a computer built between 1943 and 1945. It was used to help the US army design better weapons. Newspapers at the time called it 'a giant brain'!

ENIAC POWER

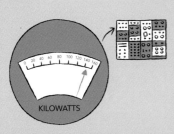

It consumed 160,000 watts of power (that's 160 kilowatts).

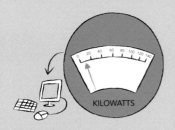

A modern computer consumes about 100 watts.

ENIAC PROCESSING

$$3 \times 5 + 2 \div 1 + 2 - 12 + 5$$

It could make 5,000 calculations per second.

$$U = \frac{1}{2} + X - \frac{dt}{dt} = \sqrt{5000-}$$
$$(1a \times 3) + D^2 + G^3 - X +$$
$$-X + Y^3 = 9.53 + \Pi - \sqrt{3.56}$$
$$2.555 - \frac{3}{100} + \sqrt{63} + T - 99$$
$$z + \frac{3}{4} + T = \sqrt{44.8-X} - (7^b$$
$$6c \times L + (E^3 + F$$

Modern supercomputers can make 93 trillion calculations per second.

Although it seems slow by today's standards, ENIAC was seen as miraculously fast in 1945. In one test, it worked out a missile's path in 30 seconds. It took a human 20 hours to make the same calculations!

73

IMPOSSIBLE INVENTIONS

Both Allied and Axis scientists came up with some
brilliantly bizarre weapons.

Bent rifle

Imagine a rifle that can
shoot round corners!
The German army invented
this curved rifle to help
infantry and tank crews
shoot around corners from a
shielded position.

handle

bent bit

Flying tank

Tanks are too heavy to fly,
right? Wrong! The Japanese
built a prototype called the
Special Number 3 Flying
Tank that could glide down
on to the battlefield and
land on a pair of skis.

sky

ground

Giant space mirror

The Nazis thought about building a huge mirror above the Earth that could concentrate the sun's rays and vaporize whole cities. Fortunately the War ended before they could build it.

Iceberg aircraft carrier

The Allies needed an aircraft base halfway across the Atlantic. They considered building a giant iceberg and using the top as a runway and the inside as an aircraft hangar. The idea was shelved in 1944 because it was getting too expensive.

PAPER POWER

The Allies dropped an estimated **6 BILLION** leaflets on Western Europe during the Second World War. This was known as the 'confetti war'.

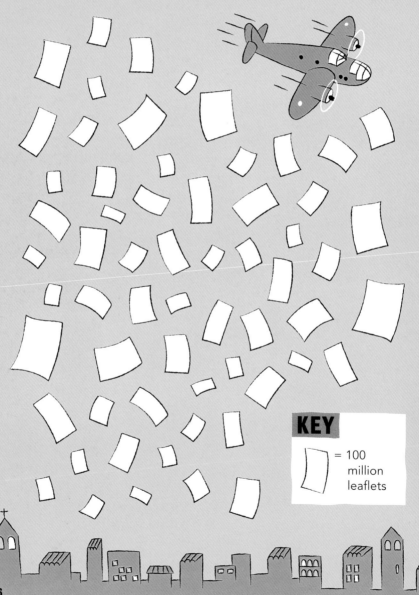

KEY

= 100 million leaflets

What did the leaflets say?

They tended to contain one of these four messages:

WARNING!

We're about to blow
everything up!
Leave this area now!

CONGRATULATIONS!

This is a surrender pass!
Hand this leaflet to one
of our soldiers and you
will not be hurt.

STOP FIGHTING!

Your leaders are liars.
Most of them have
already fled the country.
Don't die for their sake.*

HELP
HAS ARRIVED!

We've dropped food and
medical supplies in a field
outside the city. Go and
help yourself!

*These propaganda-style leaflets were often lies.

DOUBLE IDENTITY

Every great spy needs a spy name.
These real-life secret agents had courage,
cunning and **LOTS** of secret identities . . .

Actual name:

Nancy Wake

Spy names:

Lucienne Carlier
Madame Andrée

Most magnificent mission:

She was known by the Germans as the 'White Mouse', because she was impossible to catch. Wake led 7,500 French Resistance fighters in secret operations against the Germans. In one mission, she cycled 400 kilometres (250 miles) in three days to pick up a book of secret codes.

Actual name:

Krystyna Skarbek

Spy names:

Christine Granville
Madame Pauline
Madame Marchand

Most outstanding operation:

She walked into a German prison even though her 'wanted' poster was all over the Nazi headquarters. She pretended to be the niece of an important general and ordered the Nazi officer to release two British prisoners. She then walked straight out of the prison with them!

If you were a spy, it was important to **BLEND IN**. One female British spy got caught after she looked the wrong way when crossing a road in France. She'd forgotten that, while British cars drive on the left, French cars drive on the right.

Actual name:

Virginia Hall

Spy names:

Marie Monin, Germaine, Diane, Marie of Lyon, Camille, Nicolas

Most extraordinary exploit:

Considered by the Germans to be 'the most dangerous of all British spies', Virginia Hall ran secret agent networks in France. At one point, she escaped from the Germans by climbing across the Pyrenees mountains in Spain. This was in spite of the fact that she had a wooden leg (that she called 'Cuthbert').

Actual name:

Juan Pujol

Spy names:

At least 27 different identities

Most daring double-cross:

Juan Pujol (codenamed Garbo) was a British spy who played a crucial part in D-Day by feeding the Nazis false information. Pujol had convinced the Germans that he was actually 'one of their own'. Nazi agents funded Pujol's whole network, unaware that all 27 of his spies were Pujol himself!

SUPER SPY

This woman looks completely normal, right?
Let's take a closer look.

This hairbrush has
a hollow centre with
a map inside!

This button on her jacket
contains a secret compass.

British spies sent to
Spain were sometimes
given chocolate bars full
of garlic to eat, so they
blended in with the
locals (who loved garlic!).

Her right shoe
has a sliding panel
in the heel.

The pen in her jacket pocket is actually a tiny gun that can fire needles or bullets.

These chess pieces contain pellets of clothes dye. These were used to dye British uniforms to make them look German.

CHESS

These were all **ACTUAL** objects specially made for British spies in the Second World War.

MASS DECEPTION

It wasn't just people that went undercover.
Buildings and vehicles also took on new shapes.

BEFORE

The roof of Boeing's Plant
Number 2, where B-17
bombers were built.
An obvious target for
enemy bombers.

AFTER

A fake 26-acre village
complete with trees, houses
and even clothes on washing
lines. Much less of a target!

BEFORE

A field outside Bristol, four
miles from the city and one
mile from anyone's house.

AFTER

Huge strings of lights and
bonfires designed to look
like a bombed city at night,
so German planes dropped
their bombs here instead of
on Bristol!

BEFORE

An empty field in South-East England, close to Dover, with just a few sheep nibbling grass.

AFTER

Rows of inflatable tanks. This was designed to trick Hitler into thinking that the Allies were going to land at Calais – rather than Normandy.

BEFORE

A sky full of parachutists ready to land in French villages and begin the invasion of Normandy.

AFTER

500 'paradummies', full of sand and straw, designed to blow up when they hit the ground. Tape recorders on their backs played the sounds of gunfire.

RIP'S TIPS

What is camouflage?

There are two types of camouflage:
1) Making objects invisible or hard to see
2) Making objects look like something else
Both types of camouflage were used in the War.

SEEING DOUBLE

Many of the leaders employed look-a-likes to take their places – particularly in dangerous situations.

Adolf Hitler [1 double]

The German leader had at least one double: Gustav Weler. Weler is believed to have stood in for Hitler on several occasions, and reportedly died with Hitler in his bunker at the end of the War.

Bernard Montgomery [2 doubles]

Montgomery, the leader of the British army, had two doubles. One of them, Clifton James, only had four fingers, so he had to wear a fake one to make sure his hand looked like Montgomery's.

Joseph Stalin [4 doubles]

The Russian leader had at least four doubles. The most famous was Felix Dadaev, a ballet dancer and juggler, who took Stalin's place on a plane bound for the Yalta peace conference in 1945 – while Stalin followed on a later plane.

When British leader Winston Churchill sailed to Canada in 1943, the Secret Services pretended that it was actually Queen Wilhelmina of the Netherlands on board the ship. What do you think? Can you tell the difference?

Willie   **Winnie**

BRAIN FOOD

Some books needed to be destroyed after reading.

These two books on sabotage were produced by a secret British government department in 1939.

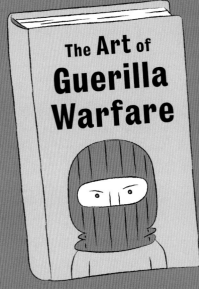

The **Partisan Leader's** Handbook

The **Art** of **Guerilla Warfare**

But they were books with a difference. They were printed on edible paper so, after reading them, you could eat them!

This was meant to take just **TWO** minutes, provided you had a glass of water to help wash them down.

(Don't try this at home! Regular books taste horrible!)

HEROES AND HEROINES

The Second World War plunged the world into six years of incredible pain and suffering. But it also turned millions of ordinary people into heroes and heroines, as they fought for their countries or tried to protect other people.

Here are just a few of their stories.

THE SHIPS OF DUNKIRK

In 1940, around 400,000 Allied soldiers were stranded on the beaches of Dunkirk in France, surrounded by the Germans, on the verge of being shot or captured. Then something extraordinary happened . . .

Over 1,000 boats appeared on the horizon. Around 700 of these were private vessels, not army ships. They were piloted by ordinary people who just wanted to help. The vessels included:

The paddle steamer the *Medway Queen*. She made a record seven trips between the British coast and Dunkirk – there and back – rescuing 7,000 men.

A small yacht called the *Sundowner*. Her captain was Charles Lightoller, who had survived the sinking of the *Titanic* in 1912.

A two-man canoe. Andrew Hetherington remembers his grandfather telling him about a neighbour who 'rowed out to Dunkirk to pick up a soldier and bring him back. When he got home, he turned around and did it again!'

Winston Churchill had only expected to rescue 45,000 soldiers. But, thanks to all of these boats, 338,000 Allied soldiers were evacuated. This enabled the British army to regroup and keep fighting the War.

There were other heroes on the beaches of Dunkirk:

The soldiers waiting on the beaches formed orderly queues – few panicked or pushed in. 'They all seemed to accept they had to wait their turn', remembers Signaller Alfred Baldwin.

RAF pilots flew up and down the beaches, shooting down over 300 German planes, even though the sky above Dunkirk was black with burning oil.

The Allied soldiers outside Dunkirk fought a brave rearguard action, keeping the German army away from the beaches. Over 60,000 of these men were killed or captured by the Germans.

Major General Harold Alexander was in charge of the evacuation. After the last ships left, he sailed along the beach in a motorboat, avoiding bullets and bombs, shouting: 'Is anybody there?' Only when he believed there was nobody left on the beaches did he also leave.

DID YOU KNOW?

British soldiers had to leave everything behind when evacuated. This included 64,000 vehicles and almost 400,000 tonnes of food and other supplies.

400,000 tonnes

=

about 40 Eiffel Towers

There were also some HEROIC survival stories.

LAST MAN HOME

Rifleman Bill Lacey wasn't rescued from the
Dunkirk beaches. But he did make it home . . .

It's 1940 and Bill Lacey is waiting
to be evacuated from Dunkirk.

When he got to the front of
the queue some medics
arrived with a stretcher.

Bill gave up his place to his
wounded comrade.

Later he remembered how he felt:

I watched the last of
the little ships sailing
away without me,
and I knew there was
no hope that there
would be any more
coming back.

But this was not the end for Bill.
He hid from the German army in
nearby woods.

He stole clothes from washing
lines and disguised himself as
a French civilian.

He couldn't speak French . . . so when locals spoke to him, he just nodded.

He drank from rivers and ate handfuls of straw covered in margarine.

His weight dropped to 45 kilograms, but he refused to give up or surrender to the Germans.

After four months, he spotted a fishing boat in a nearby harbour. He decided to try to get home.

He stole the boat when nobody was looking . . .

. . . and managed to sail it across the English Channel by himself.

More than four months after Dunkirk, Bill finally got back home. No other Brits who escaped from the Germans at Dunkirk managed to survive – just Bill. He lived until he was 91!

MILITARY EXERCISES

Escaping from a German Prisoner of War (POW) camp was almost impossible. But it didn't stop some brave soldiers from trying . . .

PSST

It is 1943 and a group of British prisoners have devised a cunning plan to escape from Stalag Luft III POW camp.

They start by building a vaulting horse out of packing cases and a sack stuffed with woodchips.

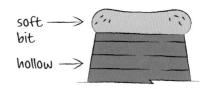

soft ⟶
bit
hollow ⟶

They ask the German guards if they can use the vaulting horse to exercise in the prison yard.
They know the Germans are keen on athletics and will say yes.

Every day four men carry the vaulting horse outside. Two prisoners have wedged themselves inside the horse.

The horse is placed roughly five metres from the fence. The prisoners do gymnastics for two to three hours, even though many have not done gymnastics for years.

One prisoner always stands by the horse. He pretends he is the coach, but **REALLY** his job is to tap on the side of the horse and warn those inside if the Germans get close.

Underneath the horse, the two men inside are digging a tunnel. They place the soil in bags suspended from a pole inside the horse.

Then comes the hard bit. After two hours, the trap door to the tunnel has to be sealed, and sand is put over it to make it look like an athletics track.

Continued . . .

The vaulting horse is carried back indoors with two men and **ALL** that heavy soil inside. The people carrying it look casual, as if it is just a light vaulting horse.

Next they get rid of the soil. They hide it everywhere: under the floor of the canteen, on the roof of the canteen, scattered in the prison gardens.

They do this every day – right under the Germans' noses – until the tunnel is 30 metres long.

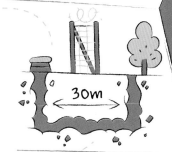

The escape is planned for 29 October 1943. Just three escapees could fit inside the horse. They are carried to the tunnel, wearing black clothing and carrying food and forged papers.

It worked! After long and difficult journeys, all three men made it back home – alive.

GREAT ESCAPES

There were other daring escape attempts from German POW camps. Five of these are real and one is made up. Can you find the **FAKE** one?

hiding in a goat's kennel

hiding under a giant heap of rubbish

dressing up as a chimney sweep, using soot to hide their face

dressing up as a Nazi and walking straight out of the gates

making a 46-metre rope out of bedsheets and copper wire

pole-vaulting over the fence using eight broomsticks tied together

Answer: These were all genuine escape attempts by Allied prisoners in German POW camps – except for the last one (pole-vaulting over the fence).

WARRIOR WOMEN

In almost every country, women played critical roles in the war: fighting, flying, nursing and much more . . .

The daring desert fighter

The Englishwoman Susan Travers was the only woman ever to serve in the French Foreign Legion. She once drove a French general out of a besieged city in North Africa, dodging tanks and machine-gun fire, making it to the British camp with the general still alive, even though her car had been hit eleven times.

The magnificent markswoman

The Soviet soldier Lyudmila Pavlichenko was perhaps the greatest sniper in history. As well as taking out almost 300 German soldiers, she was particularly skilled at one-on-one 'sniper duels', killing 36 elite enemy snipers in hunts that could last for days. Sometimes she had to remain perfectly still for 20 hours, waiting for her enemy to move.

The nurse who never gave up

Margot Turner was a British nurse stationed in South East Asia. She was evacuated during the Fall of Singapore. When her boat was sunk, she survived on a desert island for three days until being rescued. The boat that rescued her was also sunk and she survived on a raft with 16 others, nursing them as they died, until she was the only survivor. She was found by the Japanese and survived in Prisoner of War camps for three-and-a-half years in brutal conditions, taking care of her fellow prisoners until the War ended.

The perfect pilot

One of the greatest pilots who ever lived, American Jacqueline Cochran was the first woman to fly a bomber (a Lockheed Hudson V) across the Atlantic. In 1943, she persuaded the head of the US Air Corps to set up a new unit, just for female pilots. After the War, she became the first woman to break the sound barrier.

OPERATION VALKYRIE

Claus Von Stauffenberg was not a conventional hero. But if his plot to kill Hitler had succeeded, the world would have been a very different place.

This is what happened on the day of the plot, 20 July 1944.

10:00

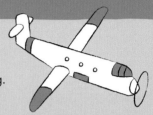

Stauffenberg and his assistant, Haeften, are on their way to 'Wolf's Lair', Hitler's heavily guarded compound in Rastenburg. They have two bombs with them.

11:00

Stauffenberg and Haeften are through the gates. They are now in the inner compound of huts and bunkers. They have a meeting with Hitler at 12:30.

12:15

The two men are directed to a waiting room. They manage to activate the first bomb, but are interrupted before they can activate the second.

12:25

On his way to the meeting with Hitler, Stauffenberg is asked twice if he'd like help carrying his case. Twice, he refuses.

FOCUS ON: Claus Von Stauffenberg

Claus Von Stauffenberg was a German army officer who hatched a plot in 1944 to try to remove Hitler from power. He had become appalled by Hitler's unpredictability and his vicious treatment of the Jews.

12:26

On arriving at the room, Stauffenberg notices that the meeting is in a wooden hut, not a concrete bunker. This means the bomb will do less damage inside the room, as the wooden hut won't contain the blast. But it's too late to turn back.

Hitler   Stauffenberg

12:27-30

Stauffenberg asks to stand near Hitler because a war injury has damaged his hearing. He is placed two seats away from Hitler.

12:30(ish)

Six minutes before the bomb is due to go off, Stauffenberg is asked to give a speech. He thought he'd have to do this later in the meeting. He stalls for a bit, then says he has an urgent phone call. He leaves his suitcase bomb behind.

The story continues . . .

12:35(ish)

After Stauffenberg leaves, German officer Colonel Brandt accidently bumps his foot on the suitcase, which moves it behind a table leg – and further away from Hitler.

12:42

Around this time, Stauffenberg hears the explosion and drives off. He assumes that Hitler is dead and Germany can end the war.

12:43

The dust clears. As the meeting was in a wooden hut and Colonel Brandt kicked the case, Hitler has escaped with only minor injuries.

The next day

Stauffenberg is arrested after a shoot-out in his offices. In spite of the fact that many German officers knew about the plot, Stauffenberg insists that it was all his own idea. He is shot the next day, on 21 July 1944.

Stauffenberg is now seen as a key figure of the German resistance: the fight against Hitler within Germany.

FIGHTING FIT

Many soldiers had injuries and disabilities, but this didn't stop them from achieving incredible feats.

Douglas Bader had two artificial legs, after having his own amputated following a plane crash. He played a leading role in the Battle of Britain and his unit claimed 62 victories. He was captured by the Germans in 1941, but managed to escape from two different prisons. In the end, the Germans threatened to confiscate his legs if he didn't stop escaping!

In the jungles of Burma, a lot of the fighting was hand-to-hand. One British soldier, George Cairns, led an attack on Pagoda Hill, even after one of his arms had just been chopped off by a samurai sword. He received the Victoria Cross – the highest award possible – for his bravery.

Claus Von Stauffenberg (see previous page) sustained a war injury that left him without a right hand and with only two fingers on his left hand. He was also blind in one eye. Yet he managed to activate a suitcase bomb that could have killed Hitler.

THE HOLOCAUST

Between 1941 and 1945, Adolf Hitler's regime murdered six million Jews, aided by fascists in France, Hungary and elsewhere.

What happened in the Holocaust?

1933 – 39

The Nazi attacks on Jews happened in stages, beginning with unfair laws that targeted Jewish people. For example, Jews were banned from schools and public places.

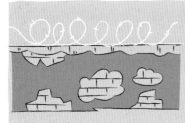

1939 – 41

Within a few years, the Nazis and their allies began to move Jewish people into ghettos, separating them from the rest of the population.

1941

Finally, the Nazis began to transport Jews to death camps such as Auschwitz and Treblinka.

As well as murdering six million Jews, the Nazis and their allies also murdered thousands of gay people, Roma and disabled people.

Most of the victims of the Holocaust had no idea they were about to be killed. The Nazis lied to them, saying they were being sent to labour camps to work.

However, some knew or suspected the truth. Here are just a few stories of remarkable courage.

Zakynthos

In 1941, the Germans occupied Greece and started rounding up Jews. On the island of Zakynthos, the German governor asked the Bishop and the Mayor of Zakynthos for a list of Jews. The Mayor and Bishop gave the governor a list with just two names on – their own. At the same time, the 275 Jews on the island were hidden in people's houses. Every Jew on Zakynthos survived the War.

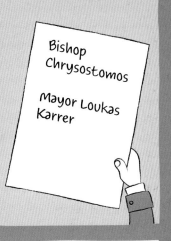

Bishop Chrysostomos

Mayor Loukas Karrer

The Bielski partisans

The Bielski partisans, led by the Bielski brothers, were a secret group of Jewish soldiers that hid out in the forests of Belorussia between 1942 and 1944. They offered food and shelter to Jews fleeing the Nazis and also attacked Nazi-controlled railways and bridges. The Germans were determined to catch them. In 1943, they sent around 20,000 soldiers to find the 700 members of the group. But the Bielski partisans

knew the forests inside out. Not only did they escape capture but they recruited even more members.

THE WARSAW GHETTO UPRISING

Between 1942 and 1943, over 300,000 Jews were deported from the Warsaw ghetto to death camps. In April 1943, the 60,000 Jews that remained rose up against the Nazis. The Nazis had tanks and automatic weapons; the Jews had sticks, homemade weapons and a few pistols. The Jews were also starving. But against all odds they fought incredibly bravely. The Nazis had hoped to clear the ghetto in three days, but it took them almost a month because of the courage of Jewish resistance fighters.

Daily food rations (in calories) in occupied Warsaw

Jews	184
Poles	669
RDA*	2,500
Germans	2,613

* Recommended daily allowance for an adult male

THE TREBLINKA UPRISING

In the Treblinka concentration camp, a group of prisoners were inspired by the Warsaw Ghetto Uprising to plan their own act of resistance. In August 1943, prisoners stole weapons and charged the gates. Around 300 prisoners escaped. The Nazis caught just over half of the escapees – the others made it to safety.

JANUS KORCZAK

Janus Korczak was the director of the orphanage in the Warsaw ghetto. When the Nazis came to take away the orphanage's 200 children, the Polish resistance told Korczak they could help him to escape. But he refused, saying his duty was to stay with the children. The Nazis also offered to smuggle him out, but again he refused. He told the orphans to put on their best clothes and pick a favourite toy or book. He walked the children to the train station, telling them it was a school trip, so they wouldn't be scared. Korczak and all the children were murdered by the Nazis at Treblinka.

The Diary of Anne Frank

If you'd like to read more incredible stories of bravery in the Holocaust, try searching online with a parent or teacher for information about Anne Frank, Oskar Schindler or the Sobibor uprising.

FAST FACTS

You've met heroes and heroines from throughout the War. Now it's time for some fast facts – the key numbers, dates and events of the Second World War. Starting with a timeline . . .

September 1939

September 1939

Germany invades Poland

By the end of the War, almost 20% of Poland's population would be dead, including at least 3 million Polish Jews.

September 1939

UK and France declare war on Germany

As well as Britain and France, their colonies and protectorates such as Australia, Canada and India also declare war on Germany.

1940

May 1940

Hitler invades France

British forces in France are evacuated from Dunkirk thanks to over 1,000 evacuation ships, including around 700 fishing boats, yachts, paddle steamers and other private vessels.

July 1940

The Battle of Britain begins

Despite being outnumbered, the British air force beat the German Luftwaffe, preventing the German invasion of Britain.

1941

June 1941

Operation Barbarossa

Hitler invades Russia with over 3 million soldiers. Russian dictator Stalin sends over 5 million soldiers to meet them. By 1945, the Eastern Front will have claimed 4 million German lives.

December 1941

Pearl Harbor

The USA enters the War after the Japanese bomb the US military base at Pearl Harbor. The Japanese deliberately attack on a Sunday and many of the US servicemen are still in their pyjamas.

January 1942

The Wannsee Conference

The Germans begin 'The Final Solution', the planned extermination of Europe's Jews, in which around 6 million Jewish people would be killed.

February 1942

Fall of Singapore

After overrunning European colonies in South East Asia, including French Indochina and Burma, the Japanese take Singapore.

August 1942 – Feb 1943

The Battle of Stalingrad

The Red Army of Russia lose more soldiers at the Battle of Stalingrad than the US Armed Forces lose in the entire war. But they eventually defeat the Germans.

October – November 1942

Battle of El Alamein

This battle in the North African desert was the first British victory over the German army. It forced the Germans to retreat 1,500 miles from Egypt to Tunisia.

1943

July 1943

The Allies land on Sicily

Around 478,000 Allied soldiers land on the island of Sicily, and the liberation of Italy begins.

1944

June 1944

D-Day landings

In the largest seaborne invasion in history, over 160,000 Allied troops land in Normandy, France on a single day, 6 June 1944. The Germans are pushed back across Northern France.

1945

April – May 1945

Battle of Berlin

Soviet troops capture Berlin. Hitler commits suicide and the Germans surrender.

September 1945

Japanese surrender

The US drops a nuclear bomb on Hiroshima in Japan, killing 70,000 people instantly. Thousands more die later of radiation poisoning. A second nuclear bomb is dropped on Nagasaki, and the Japanese surrender.

September 1945

CASUALTIES AND DEATHS

Over 20,000 people were killed on each day of the Second World War (1939 – 45). Or, to put it another way, every five minutes, 70 people lost their lives.

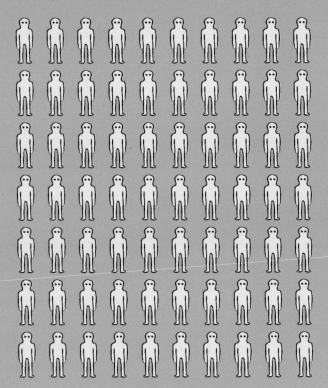

Civilian casualties

WWI

In the Second World War, two thirds (66%) of casualties were ordinary civilians, not soldiers. This made it very different from previous wars. For example, in the First World War, just 5% of casualties were civilians – the rest were soldiers, sailors and pilots.

WW II

Military deaths in WWII (1939 – 45)

Soviet Union	10.7 million
Germany	5.5 million
China	3.8 million
Japan	2.1 million
Britain and Commonwealth	575,000
USA	417,000
Italy	301,000
France	218,000
Poland	160,000
Others	1.4 million

Civilian deaths (1937 – 45)

China	16.2 million
Soviet Union	12.4 million
Poland	5.4 million
Germany	1.8 million
Britain and Commonwealth	1.6 million
Japan	1 million
France	350,000
Italy	150,000
Others	8.5 million

1 in 4 Belarusians died

In terms of percentage of population, Eastern Europe suffered the most. 25% of the population of Belarus, and almost 20% of the population of Poland and the Ukraine died. In total, about 3% of the world's population died in World War Two.

Winston Churchill

Role: British Prime Minister

Age in 1939: 64

Random fact: As well as being a great leader, he also invented the 'onesie' or romper suit. He often wore onesies at important meetings with other world leaders.

Franklin D. Roosevelt

Role: US President

Age in 1939: 58

Random fact: In 1921, an illness left him paralysed from the waist down. However, he tried to hide this, and had iron braces fitted to his legs to make it look like he could stand without assistance.

Adolf Hitler

Role: German leader (he called himself 'Führer', which means 'leader')

Age in 1939: 50

Random fact: As well as being vicious and violent, Hitler was also vain. He was short-sighted but thought glasses made him look weak, so all his speeches had to be printed with huge letters – like a baby book!

Benito Mussolini

Role: Italian leader (he called himself 'Duce', which means 'leader')

Age in 1939: 56

Random fact: He was expelled from his religious boarding school for stabbing another pupil. He later went on to qualify as a teacher!

Joseph Stalin

Role: Premier of the Soviet Union

Age in 1939: 60

Random fact: One of the reasons that the Soviet Union struggled at the start of the war is that Stalin had killed most of the army leaders because he thought they were plotting against him. Only 22 out of 103 military chiefs were still alive by 1939.

Hirohito

Role: Japanese Emperor

Age in 1939: 38

Random fact: When Hirohito read out the Japanese surrender on the radio in 1945, it was the first time the Japanese people had ever heard his voice. Hirohito lived for another 44 years after the end of the War.

Other key figures include General De Gaulle (France), Mao Tse-Tung (China), General MacArthur (US General), General Patton (US General), Field Marshal Montgomery (UK) and Nazis such as Joseph Goebbels and Heinrich Himmler.

PUFFIN BOOKS

UK | USA | Canada | Ireland | Australia
India | New Zealand | South Africa

Puffin Books is part of the Penguin Random House group of companies
whose addresses can be found at global.penguinrandomhouse.com.

www.penguin.co.uk   www.puffin.co.uk   www.ladybird.co.uk

First published 2019
001

Text and illustrations copyright © Penguin Books Ltd, 2019

Text by Adam Frost
Illustrations by Daniel Limon

Printed in Malaysia

A CIP catalogue record for this book is available from the British Library

ISBN: 978-0-241-35148-2

All correspondence to:
Puffin Books, Penguin Random House Children's
80 Strand, London WC2R 0RL

Photographs on page 2 courtesy of Imperial War Museums © IWM (D 5950) and © IWM (D 5937)

Author's Note:

This book would not have been possible without hundreds of brilliant books, magnificent museums
and wonderful websites. All the sources I used are here: **bit.ly/2ndWorldWar**

A lot of the books I used are written for adults, so please check with your parents or teachers before
you start reading them.

Some great books for children include:
World War Two: The Definitive Visual Guide, Richard Holmes (2015); Introduction to the Second
World War, Paul Dowswell (2005); Blitzed Brits, Terry Deary (2012); Weird War Two, Peter Taylor
(2017); True Stories of the Second World War, Henry Brook and Paul Dowswell (IWM, 2007)

Great museums to visit include:
The Imperial War Museum, London; The Imperial War Museum, Duxford; The Royal Air Force
Museum, Cosford; The Churchill War Rooms, London